FRIENDSHIP
Iron Sharpening Iron

JUNE HUNT

Friendship: Iron Sharpening Iron
Copyright © 2014 Hope For The Heart
Aspire Press is an imprint of
Rose Publishing, LLC
P.O. Box 3473
Peabody, Massachusetts 01961-3473 USA
www.hendricksonrose.com

For more information on Hope For The Heart, visit www.hopefortheheart.org or call 1-800-488-HOPE (4673).

Printed in the United States of America

December 2017, 5th printing

CONTENTS

Definitions.. 10
  What Is a Friend?.................................... 10
  What Is Friendship?................................. 12
  What Is a Codependent Friendship? 14
  What Is the Value of Vulnerability
    in Friendships? 17

Characteristics of Friendships............... 21
  What Are the Three Levels of Friendship? 21
  What Friendships Did Jesus Establish?............ 24
  What Characterizes Negative and
    Positive Friendships?......................... 27
  What Does a Codependent Friendship
    Look Like?... 29
  What Do Healthy Friendships Look
    Like in Families?............................... 32
  What Do Unhealthy Family Friendships
    Look Like?... 35

Causes of Failed Friendships 38
  Why Does Selfishness Sabotage Friendships?.... 39
  Why Do Friends Fall into Manipulation?........ 42
  Why Are There Barriers to Intimacy
    within Friendships?........................... 46
  Root Cause of Unfulfilled Friendships............. 48

Steps to Solution.. 53
  How to Initiate Possible Friendships................. 56
  How to Reach Out and Be a Friend 59
  How to Fan the Flame of Friendship............... 63

How to Listen and Liberate a Friend 68

How to Move toward Intimacy 71

How to Commit to Intimacy in Friendship 74

How to Communicate to Form and
    Further Friendships 76

How to Find Freedom from a
    Codependent Friendship 78

How to Build Healthy Boundaries 86

How to Paint a Scriptural Portrait of
    Faithful Friends 89

Dear Friend,

I know what it's like to *not have a friend*—a true friend, a trusted confidant. And for good reason. I couldn't share my painful home life with anyone. I felt like there was a cork in my throat.

In reality, I grew up in an adulterous home—off on the side. Then after my dad's first wife died, our family of five moved into his huge house. (I was 12 years old.) A year later, my parents married.

During this period, an unspoken code of "family loyalty" prevented me from trusting others with the truth. Oh, I had acquaintances. But they weren't aware of the embarrassing secrets locked behind our closed doors and my closed heart. Secrecy and shame were my only intimate companions.

Then in 11th grade, I met Catherine. Reserved and winsome, Catherine's sensitive nature seemed to parallel my own. She was a senior who had just moved to town (how hard was that!). Quite soon, Catherine was the answer to my unspoken prayer. Finally, I had my first friend!

As I poured out my heart to her, family secrets, personal pain, and private thoughts cascaded out like an undammed river.

After Catherine left for college the following fall, I could hardly wait to see her smiling face at Christmas. However, following her return Catherine explained that she had outgrown our friendship and needed to "move on." Then she suggested I do the same. In social media terms, she "unfriended" me (though the term didn't exist back then). Absolutely crushed, I reluctantly parted company with my first friend.

Nevertheless, in following years, the Lord began to bring new friends into my life—a small group of "forever friends" who have literally stood by me in the good times and the bad. Through this process I began to see that, just as Jesus had chosen disciples whom He called "friends"—we can have an inner circle of friends—not a cast of forty, but a few close friends.

Instead of focusing on one exclusive friend, how much better to have a "family of friends" that resides within the home of our hearts. In this "home," each friend occupies their own special place and each fulfills a special, meaningful purpose. For example, the warm inviting living room where laughter and entertainment abounds is quite different from the cozy comfort of the kitchen table where stomachs and hearts are nourished. Even two necessary rooms, the laundry room and the bedroom, can never take the place of the other. In my "Friendship House," my *grace friend*, Barbara (who taught me grace), doesn't occupy the same space as my *ethics friend*, Eleanor. And my *ready-to-go friend*, June, inhabits a different place in my heart than my *"you light up my life" friend*, Sue. One room—or one friend—can never take the place of another.

I love the word *friend*. A friend is not your judge and jury. A friend holds your hurting heart.

A friend is "iron that sharpens iron" to bring out your best. Whatever your friend says and does is born out of love, not to shut you up or tear you down. As Proverbs 27:17 says, *"As iron sharpens iron, so one man sharpens another."* That's the heart of friendship.

My precious *forever friend*, Sue, now at home with the Lord, gave me a stained glass etching with these words: *"A friend is someone to whom you can pour out all the contents of your heart—chaff and grain together—knowing that the gentlest of hands will take and sift it, keep what is worth keeping and with the breath of kindness blow the rest away."* How I've loved that sentiment and how I loved having her as my friend.

Years ago, my excruciating experience with Catherine did make me cautious (Proverbs 12:26), but it also heightened my value of friendship, teaching me to never take for granted God's priceless gift of a friend.

Instead of focusing on *getting* friendship, God calls us to focus on *giving* friendship. Our joy and significance will be found in serving and befriending others as an extension of the Lord's love for us. (See John 15:10–12.)

The source of rich, godly friendships is God, Himself. James 1:17 says, *"Every good and perfect gift is from above."* If you seek abiding friendships, if you have a need for closeness and intimacy, ask God to bring wise friends into your life who will take Him seriously. Ask for friends who will esteem Him and who are committed to Him. As you pray, begin reaching out and serving others by being a friend. As you do, may the *biblical hope and practical help* in this book guide you in your quest for *"a friend who sticks closer than a brother"* (Proverbs 18:24).

Yours in the Lord's hope,

June Hunt

FRIENDSHIP
Iron Sharpening Iron

Imagine a young man who has it all. He comes from a powerful family and is heir apparent to the family fortune. Everyone knows that one day he is destined to take his father's place as head of the business. Fortunately, he has the temperament and giftedness to fill his father's shoes.

Yet this talented son is willing to sacrifice everything for another capable man—his closest friend whom he believes is the right choice to run the empire. Where there could be contention, there is instead undying commitment. His extraordinary decision is unprecedented—unparalleled. Where there could be rivalry, there is genuine respect. In truth, David is God's anointed, and his friend Jonathan does everything possible to support the one who will rightfully rule, including protecting David from his own jealous father, the reigning King of Israel.

Jonathan is willing to sacrifice everything—even the throne—for the higher good of his friend. He enters into a covenant friendship with the man God has chosen as king, and he intends for their sworn oath of friendship to have an impact for generations to come.

**"Jonathan said to David,
'Whatever you want me to do, I'll do for you."
(1 Samuel 20:4)**

DEFINITIONS

Earlier, Jonathan must have at least known of David—he served in the palace courts and had quite the reputation. One man in the palace said, *"I have seen a son of Jesse of Bethlehem who knows how to play the harp. He is a brave man and a warrior. He speaks well and is a fine-looking man. And the LORD is with him"* (1 Samuel 16:18).

But the day David slew the giant Goliath, whatever limited relationship he and Jonathan may have had deepened dramatically to what can only be characterized as diehard devotion. That very day a strong spiritual bond suddenly connected the two young men in deepest friendship.

> **"Jonathan became one in spirit with David, and he loved him as himself. ...
> And Jonathan made a covenant with David because he loved him as himself."
> (1 Samuel 18:1, 3)**

WHAT IS a Friend?

Like father, *unlike son.*

Saul and Jonathan cannot be more different in their attitudes and actions toward David. Although David has brought honor to the king through one military victory after another, it is the refrain of a song that galls Saul and has him seeing green where David is concerned. The words credit Saul with slaying thousands, but David with tens of thousands. *"And from that time on Saul kept a jealous eye on David"* (1 Samuel 18:9).

Jonathan reveres David, Saul reviles him. Soon Saul's emotions churn with murderous hatred and the maniacal monarch attempts to kill David, time and time again. So while Saul seeks to take David's life, Jonathan seeks to protect it. Jonathan's commitment to the will of God and to the bond of friendship is far stronger than the blood tie of his father. There could not be a more devoted friend than Jonathan. But what does it mean to be a friend?

▶ **A friend** is a person united to another by feelings of affection, loyal support, and time spent together.[1]

▶ *Friend* translated in the Greek is *philos*, which is a term of endearment.[2]

- *Philadelphia* means "brotherly love."[3]
- *Philanthropy* means the love for man, benevolence.[4]

Jesus said...

"Greater love has no one than this, that he lay down his life for his friends" (John 15:13).

▶ **Friend** developed from the Old English word *freond*, which is related to the Old English word *freon*, which means "to love."[5] Thus the basis for genuine friendship is love.

The Bible reminds us ...

> **"A friend loves at all times."**
> **(Proverbs 17:17)**

WHAT IS Friendship?[6]

David becomes a man on the run from Saul. Caught up in the terrors of the moment, his prior anointing as the next king of Israel by the prophet Samuel is, no doubt, a distant memory. Before beginning life as a fugitive, David and Jonathan exchange a grievous, gut-wrenching farewell: *"David ... bowed down before Jonathan three times, with his face to the ground. Then they kissed each other and wept together—but David wept the most"* (1 Samuel 20:41).

Jonathan told David: *"Go in peace, for we have sworn friendship with each other in the name of the Lord, saying, 'The Lord is witness between you and me, and between your descendants and my descendants forever'"* (1 Samuel 20:42).

▶ **Friendship** is a reciprocal relationship of liking and loving between two people.

▶ **Friendship** is a mutual emotion based on liking—*phileo* love.

- The Greek word *phileo* means "tender affection."[7]

- Because of Abraham's faithfulness to the Lord, he was given the unique title "the friend of God," a *philos* of God, not a *hetairos* of God.

"The scripture was fulfilled that says, 'Abraham believed God, and it was credited to him as righteousness,' and he was called God's friend" (James 2:23).

▶ **Friendship** that is mature also includes *agape* love.

■ The Greek word *agape* means a commitment to seek the highest good of another, even when a person has characteristics you don't like.

"God demonstrates his own love for us in this: While we were still sinners, Christ died for us" (Romans 5:8).

Reporting a Friend

QUESTION: "Was I wrong to report my friend for being on drugs and possibly hurting his child? He refuses to have anything to do with me now, and I really miss him."

ANSWER: No, out of concern for both your friend and his child, you were not wrong to report your friend. To the contrary, you were right in seeking to protect him from himself and to protect his child from possible injury.

Obviously, your friend needs help. Helping a friend who puts others at risk means holding your friend accountable. Sometimes we are led by God to do something that causes our loved ones to suffer a little now so that they won't suffer a lot later. Your decision was right because:

- ▶ **You tried to save your friend** from doing something that could possibly harm his relationship with his son for the rest of his life.

- ▶ **You stepped in and spared him** from doing something he could regret forever.

- ▶ **Your action was that of a true friend**—doing what is in the best interest of another regardless of how that person responds.

Pray that, in time, God will use your intervention to open the eyes of your friend and to serve as a catalyst for him to change.

> **"Better is open rebuke than hidden love.**
> **Wounds from a friend can be trusted,**
> **but an enemy multiplies kisses."**
> **(Proverbs 27:5–6)**

WHAT IS a Codependent Friendship?[8]

In the strictest sense of the word, there are no codependent *friendships* because friends are committed to doing what is best and right for one another, and fostering codependency is both wrong and hurtful. We are to lock hands in friendship and look to God in dependency—trusting Him and deriving our strength from Him.

The Bible says, *"He gives strength to the weary and increases the power of the weak."* (Isaiah 40:29)

▶ **Codependent enablers** are those who enable addicts or the dysfunctional people in their lives to continue with their addictions or dysfunctionality without drawing and maintaining boundaries.

▶ **Codependent people** are those who are dependent on another person to the point of being controlled or manipulated by that person. Just as the alcoholic is dependent on alcohol, the codependent is dependent on being needed by the alcoholic or on being needed by someone who is problematic.

▶ **Codependency** is a relationship addiction comparable to the sin of depending on false gods that are powerless to help or depending on a broken water well that won't hold water. It simply won't work! God pointed out this fact in referencing the Israelites: *"My people have committed two sins: They have forsaken me, the spring of living water, and have dug their own cisterns, broken cisterns that cannot hold water"* (Jeremiah 2:13).

Enabling

QUESTION: **"How can I know whether or not I'm an enabler?"**

ANSWER: You are an enabler if you perpetuate another's destructive behavior by protecting that person from painful consequences that could actually serve as a motivation for change.

Ask yourself, *How many lies have I told to protect the reputation of someone with a destructive habit?*

The Bible has strong words to say about those who protect the guilty:

> **"Whoever says to the guilty,
> 'You are innocent'—peoples will curse him
> and nations denounce him."
> (Proverbs 24:24)**

Biblical Dependency

QUESTION: "What is biblical dependency?"

ANSWER: God did not create us to be dependent or codependent on others, but He did create us in such a way that we must depend on Him, not just to meet our three basic needs for love, significance, and security but also for life itself![9] Therefore ...

▶ **God wants you to depend on Him**—to totally rely on Him, not on people or things or self-effort. Scripture says ...

"My salvation and my honor depend on God; he is my mighty rock, my refuge" (Psalm 62:7).

▶ **God wants you to depend on Him**—to believe that He will meet all of your needs. You can safely reveal your hurts, your fears, and your needs to God. He will be your Need-Meeter. Scripture says ...

"The LORD will guide you always; he will satisfy your needs in a sun-scorched land and will

strengthen your frame. You will be like a well-watered garden, like a spring whose waters never fail" (Isaiah 58:11).

▶ **God wants you to depend on Him**—to trust in Him to take care of your loved ones. Scripture says ...

"Trust in him at all times, O people; pour out your hearts to him, for God is our refuge" (Psalm 62:8).

▶ **God wants you to depend on Him**—to rely on Christ, whose life in you will enable you to overcome any destructive dependency. Scripture says ...

"The one [Christ] who is in you is greater than the one [Satan] who is in the world" (1 John 4:4).

WHAT IS the Value of Vulnerability in Friendships?

Every level of friendship requires a certain amount of disclosure, but deep, close friendships require personal disclosure to the point of becoming *vulnerable* to one another. *Vulnerability* means being susceptible to physical, emotional, or spiritual injury, risking greater repercussion for greater reward. In friendship, the vulnerable heart can either be greatly helped or greatly hurt.

"To the weak I became weak, to win the weak. I have become all things to all men so that by all possible means I might save some." (1 Corinthians 9:22)

Vulnerability is ...

▶ **Courageously choosing** to be completely honest in all circumstances.

"An honest answer is like a kiss on the lips" (Proverbs 24:26).

▶ **Courageously confessing** when you are wrong.

"When a man or woman wrongs another in any way and so is unfaithful to the LORD, that person is guilty and must confess the sin he has committed" (Numbers 5:6–7).

▶ **Courageously receiving** guidance.

"Let the wise listen and add to their learning, and let the discerning get guidance" (Proverbs 1:5).

▶ **Courageously accepting** advice and instruction.

"Listen to advice and accept instruction, and in the end you will be wise" (Proverbs 19:20).

Vulnerability in a friendship means being open enough with one another to create the possibility of receiving greater pleasure or greater pain resulting in greater love or greater loss.[10] Such interaction involves ...

▶ **Courageously sharing** your painful past and present struggles.

"Confess your sins to each other and pray for each other so that you may be healed. The prayer of a righteous man is powerful and effective" (James 5:16).

▶ **Courageously stating** your self-doubts and secret desires.

"God can testify how I long for all of you with the affection of Christ Jesus" (Philippians 1:8).

▶ **Courageously speaking** of your strong beliefs and spiritual values.

"Always be prepared to give an answer to everyone who asks you to give the reason for the hope that you have. But do this with gentleness and respect" (1 Peter 3:15).

▶ **Courageously seeking** honest evaluation of your personal strengths and weaknesses.

"I did not come with eloquence or superior wisdom as I proclaimed to you the testimony about God. ... I came to you in weakness and fear, and with much trembling. My message and my preaching were not with wise and persuasive words, but with a demonstration of the Spirit's power" (1 Corinthians 2:1, 3–4).

Vulnerability in your friendship with God implies a willingness to open up to Him by ...

▶ **Courageously confessing** your toughest temptations.

"I confess my iniquity; I am troubled by my sin" (Psalm 38:18).

▶ **Courageously communicating** your troublesome thoughts.

"The troubles of my heart have multiplied; free me from my anguish" (Psalm 25:17).

"But I call to God, and the L<small>ORD</small> *saves me. Evening, morning and noon I cry out in distress, and he* [God] *hears my voice"* (Psalm 55:16–17).

▶ **Courageously conveying** your angry attitudes.

"Jonah was greatly displeased and became angry. ... God said to Jonah, 'Do you have a right to be angry about the vine?' 'I do,' he said. 'I am angry enough to die'" (Jonah 4:1, 9).

▶ **Courageously confiding** your locked-away longings.

"All my longings lie open before you, O L<small>ORD</small>; *my sighing is not hidden from you"* (Psalm 38:9).

Of course, regardless of what we think is hidden from God, the Bible says ...

"Nothing in all creation is hidden from God's sight. Everything is uncovered and laid bare before the eyes of him to whom we must give account."
(Hebrews 4:13)

CHARACTERISTICS OF FRIENDSHIPS

Jonathan and Saul also become men on the run, fleeing the nation of Israel's fierce enemy—the Philistines. The king and his three sons become key targets of the pagan warriors, and before long the inner royal circle is destroyed. Sadly, Jonathan is killed along with his brothers, and Saul is critically wounded and commits suicide to avoid falling into enemy hands.

With Jonathan dead, the cherished covenant between he and David will soon be enacted for the next generation. David said, *"I will surely show you kindness for the sake of your father Jonathan"* (2 Samuel 9:7).

WHAT ARE the Three Levels of Friendship?[11]

It can only be characterized as the most committed of friendships. The death of Jonathan plunges David into a grief-filled season of mourning, weeping, and fasting. The soon-to-be-king orders that a lament be taught to the men of Judah, one honoring both Jonathan and Saul for their contributions to the nation. But for Jonathan, David reserves the most tender words of all in tribute to the impact of steadfast, sacrificial love. *"I grieve for you, Jonathan my brother; you were very dear to me. Your love for me was wonderful, more wonderful than that of women"* (2 Samuel 1:26).

Jonathan had implored David in a covenant promise, *"do not ever cut off your kindness from my family"* (1 Samuel 20:15). Once the newly crowned king consolidates his kingdom and conquers his enemies, his faithfulness to the friendship covenant is manifested with a question: *"Is there anyone still left of the house of Saul to whom I can show kindness for Jonathan's sake?"* (2 Samuel 9:1).

While Jonathan and David shared a deep, committed friendship, some relationships operate on a more shallow level.

CASUAL FRIENDS

These are the people with whom you have ...

▶ Occasional contact

▶ Common interests and activities

▶ Some knowledge of accomplishments, abilities, and character qualities

▶ Concern for personal problems

▶ Guarded emotions

▶ No accountability

**"I hope to see you soon,
and we will talk face to face. Peace to you.
The friends here send their greetings.
Greet the friends there by name."
(3 John 14)**

Close Friends

These are the people with whom you have ...

▶ Regular contact

▶ Mutual interests and activities

▶ Sensitivity to likes, dislikes, strengths, and weaknesses

▶ Personal comfort during trials and sorrows

▶ Willingness to become vulnerable

▶ Limited accountability

> "Do two walk together unless
> they have agreed to do so?"
> (Amos 3:3)

Committed Friends

These are the people with whom you have ...

▶ Made a commitment to spend quality time together

▶ Shared values and goals, joys and sorrows, experiences and commitments

▶ Freedom to help correct character flaws

▶ Personal involvement in defending reputation

▶ Frequently risked transparency

▶ Reciprocal commitment with sacrificial love

"Ruth replied [to Naomi], 'Don't urge me to leave you or to turn back from you. Where you go I will go, and where you stay I will stay. Your people will be my people and your God my God. Where you die I will die, and there I will be buried. May the Lᴏʀᴅ deal with me, be it ever so severely, if anything but death separates you and me.'"
(Ruth 1:16–17)

WHAT FRIENDSHIPS Did Jesus Establish?

The friendships of Jesus can best be described by three concentric circles.

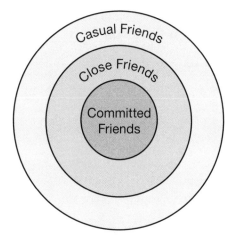

The outer circle consists of large crowds of people who follow Jesus, containing both believers and unbelievers. The Pharisees label Jesus *"a friend*

of tax collectors and 'sinners'" (Luke 7:34), and these are the outer ring of people to whom Jesus brings redemption and blessing and with whom He establishes *casual* friendships.

The middle circle is comprised of people with whom Jesus spends more time and shares more experiences. Eight of his 12 apostles, plus three siblings—Mary, Martha, and Lazarus—are all *close* friends of Jesus. These apostles witness miracle after miracle. And alongside these two sisters, they watch Jesus raise Lazarus from the dead.

The inner circle of *committed* friendships is reserved for a trio from within the 12—Peter, James, and John. They are continually with Jesus when He displays supernatural power, as well as when He experiences incredible pain. It is these three who are privileged to get a glimpse of Jesus' glory when He is transfigured before them in dazzling array. And it is Peter, James, and John whom Jesus takes with Him to the Garden of Gethsemane where He pours out His heart to the Father, asking that the cup of crucifixion pass from Him. Jesus allowed them to be in the inmost circle of His heart.

> "Then Jesus went with his disciples to a place called Gethsemane, and he said to them, 'Sit here while I go over there and pray.' He took Peter and the two sons of Zebedee along with him, and he began to be sorrowful and troubled."
> (Matthew 26:36–37)

Thus, apart from the general crowd and mere acquaintances, Jesus had three levels of friends.

▶ **Casual** friendships

- Certain followers of Jesus
- Tax collectors and other sinners

The Bible says, *"The Son of Man came eating and drinking, and you say, 'Here is a glutton and a drunkard, a friend of tax collectors and sinners'"* (Luke 7:34).

▶ **Close** friendships

- Eight of the 12 apostles (not Judas Iscariot)
- Mary, Martha, and Lazarus

The Bible says, *"I no longer call you servants, because a servant does not know his master's business. Instead, I have called you friends, for everything that I learned from my Father I have made known to you"* (John 15:15).

▶ **Committed** friendships

- Peter
- James
- John

The Bible says, *"Jesus took with him Peter, James and John the brother of James, and led them up a high mountain by themselves"* (Matthew 17:1).

"He took Peter, James and John along with him, and he began to be deeply distressed and troubled" (Mark 14:33).

WHAT CHARACTERIZES Negative and Positive Friendships?

No one signs up to be in a negative friendship. We all want our friendships to be positive. Sadly, many people don't know how to recognize dysfunctional characteristics simply because they grow up in a dysfunctional home around dysfunctional people. That is why we need to be discerning before getting into a friendship, because the Bible says ...

"Bad company corrupts good character."
(1 Corinthians 15:33)

The following is a list of characteristics found in negative and positive friendships.

NEGATIVE FRIENDSHIPS	POSITIVE FRIENDSHIPS
Neglects quality time with you	Commits to quality time with you
Repeatedly criticizes your weaknesses	Repeatedly compliments your strengths
Shares your secrets	Keeps your confidences
Doesn't care about your cares	Cares about your cares
Prevents your freedom through possessiveness	Promotes your freedom without possessiveness

Negative Friendships	Positive Friendships
Jealous and controlling of you	Not jealous or controlling of you
Unwilling to hear your correction	Willing to hear your correction
Focuses on your faults	Forgives your faults
Inconsistent with you	Consistent with you
Depletes your energy	Enhances your energy
Disloyal/unfaithful to you	Loyal/faithful to you
Dependent on you	Interdependent with you
Judgmental of you	Nonjudgmental of you
Discourages you	Encourages you
Readily rejects your viewpoints	Readily listens to your viewpoints
Withholds innermost thoughts and feelings	Shares innermost thoughts and feelings
Distrusts your motives	Trusts your motives
Noncommittal in your relationship	Committed to your relationship
Enables unhealthy behavior	Challenges unhealthy behavior
Listens in order to argue and defend	Listens to hear and understand

NEGATIVE FRIENDSHIPS	POSITIVE FRIENDSHIPS
Insensitive to your needs	Sensitive to your needs
Spiritually dead	Spiritually alive

Scripture admonishes you to ...

▶ *"Watch out for those who cause divisions and put obstacles in your way that are contrary to the teaching you have learned. Keep away from them"* (Romans 16:17).

▶ *"Let us consider how we may spur one another on toward love and good deeds"* (Hebrews 10:24).

WHAT DOES a Codependent Friendship Look Like?

Are you unsure about the quality of relationship you have with someone significant in your life? Is it possible you are in a relationship others would call "codependent"? If so, how would you know? Ask yourself ...

> "Am I now trying to win the
> approval of men, or of God?
> Or am I trying to please men?
> If I were still trying to please men,
> I would not be a servant of Christ."
> (Galatians 1:10)

The Codependency Checklist Test

Read through the Codependency Checklist and check (✓) everything that applies to you.

☐ Do you struggle with feeling loved, and therefore you look for ways to be needed?

☐ Do you throw *all of your energy* into helping another person?

☐ Do you say *no* when you should say *yes* and *yes* when you should say *no*?

☐ Do you feel compelled to take charge of another person's crisis?

☐ Do you feel drawn to a person whom you think needs to be rescued?

☐ Do you have difficulty setting boundaries with another person and keeping them?

☐ Do you find it difficult to identify and express your true feelings?

☐ Do you rely on another person to make most of the decisions?

☐ Do you feel lonely, sad, and empty when you are alone?

☐ Do you feel threatened when the person closest to you spends time with someone else?

☐ Do you think another person's opinions are more important than your opinions?

☐ Do you refrain from speaking in order to keep peace?

- ☐ Do you fear conflict because it could cause you to be abandoned?
- ☐ Do you become defensive about your relationship with another person?
- ☐ Do you feel "stuck" in your relationship with another person?
- ☐ Do you feel you have lost your personal identity in order to "fit into" another person's world?
- ☐ Do you feel controlled and manipulated by another person?
- ☐ Do you feel used and taken advantage of by another person?
- ☐ Do you plan your life around another person?
- ☐ Do you prioritize your relationship with another person over your relationship with the Lord?

If you responded with a *yes* to four or more of these questions, you may be involved in a codependent relationship!

When we find ourselves in unhealthy patterns of relating, we need to change our focus, change our goals, and change what is hindering us from running the race God has planned for us. Our primary focus should be not on another person but on Jesus.

> "Let us throw off everything that hinders and the sin that so easily entangles, and let us run with perseverance the race marked out for us." (Hebrews 12:1)

God created the family to provide the framework for us to learn about relationships—how to relate to one another. Those first relationships often affect how we communicate and establish friendships for the remainder of our lives.

The Bible says God intended parents to instill in their children the truths of His Word so that each succeeding generation would learn—first and foremost—how to have a healthy relationship with Him.

"God created man in his own image, in the image of God he created him; male and female he created them. God blessed them and said to them, 'Be fruitful and increase in number; fill the earth and subdue it'" (Genesis 1:27–28).

"He decreed statutes ... which he commanded our forefathers to teach their children, so the next generation would know them, even the children yet to be born, and they in turn would tell their children" (Psalm 78:5–6).

▶ The Husband/Wife Friendship

The marriage relationship forms the foundation for the family. When it is built on love, trust, and acceptance, that spirit carries down throughout the entire family. Some couples become each other's *best friends*, modeling for their children that spouses can be the closest of friends. Their love is contagious to others around them.

As friends they ...

- *Thrive* on each other's unconditional love
- *Talk* to one another in a spirit of mutual respect
- *Tackle* tough issues together, not "sweep them under the rug"

In essence, they model love to the whole family.

"Love is patient, love is kind. It does not envy, it does not boast, it is not proud. It is not rude, it is not self-seeking, it is not easily angered, it keeps no record of wrongs. Love does not delight in evil but rejoices with the truth. It always protects, always trusts, always hopes, always perseveres. Love never fails" (1 Corinthians 13:4–8).

▶ The Parent/Child Friendship

If the husband and wife each understand and fulfill their role and responsibilities with love and understanding, then there is order and structure when children enter the family because boundaries are defined. Then after moving from childhood into adulthood many mature, grown children experience a change of relationship—they become valued friends of their parents. As friends they ...

- *Dedicate* their lives to the Lord to do what is best on behalf of each other
- *Demonstrate* unconditional love for each other
- *Determine* to offer help when—but only when—help is needed and wanted

In essence, they provide living proof of the truth that, *"No discipline seems pleasant at the time, but painful. Later on, however, it produces a harvest of righteousness and peace for those who have been trained by it"* (Hebrews 12:11).

▶ The Sibling Friendship

When siblings are raised in a home with unconditional love and where discipline is applied in love, children thrive. They don't feel the need to compete for their parents' love because they each feel loved for the unique person God created them to be. In this atmosphere, they are trained to appreciate the special gifts in each other and can become *lifelong friends*. As friends, they ...

- *Care* for one another and aren't afraid to show it
- *Communicate* authentically, even about difficult issues
- *Cherish* each other's individuality

In essence, they follow the example of Christ and are identified with Him.

"By this all men will know that you are my disciples, if you love one another" (John 13:35).

▶ The Extended Family Friendship

It has been said that "blood is thicker than water." Family ties are often stronger than the ties between friends. We usually don't choose our extended family members, but we can choose whether we will learn to love them or not. Solomon says we all yearn for *hesed*—the Hebrew word for "unfailing love." We desire the kindness of friends combined with the permanence of family. As friends, they ...

- *Learn* to love one another
- *Listen* to each other in a spirit of trust
- *Lean* on one another in times of trouble

In essence, they demonstrate their understanding that, *"What a man desires is unfailing love"* (Proverbs 19:22).

WHAT DO Unhealthy Family Friendships Look Like?

In unhealthy families, there is not a secure foundation of unconditional love and acceptance. There is a spirit of competition for limited affection and a hunger for acceptance. Because members of the family have trouble loving each other, it is unlikely that a spirit of friendship can develop between family members.

▶ The Husband/Wife Relationship

The marriage relationship permeates the entire family, affecting everyone in it either for good or for bad. Couples who create contention rather than cooperation, and discouragement rather than encouragement, set the stage for their children to form unhealthy friendships as well. In an unhealthy marriage, couples ...

- *Refrain* from expressing love and kindness to one another

- *Reproach* each other in public
- *React* to the tiniest of offenses and keep account of them

In essence, they model division and disharmony to the whole family.

"If a house is divided against itself, that house cannot stand" (Mark 3:25).

▶ The Parent/Child Relationship

Healthy boundaries are essential for creating a home in which each person feels loved, affirmed, and secure. Some parents fear that if they become too strict and put up boundary lines, then their children will not love them. Their fear of losing their child's love causes them to try to create a friendship, rather than a healthy parent/child relationship. As their child's supposed "friend," they ...

- *Coddle* their children instead of establishing boundaries
- *Choose* to be "buddies," rather than to parent appropriately
- *Criticize* their children often and in front of others

In essence, rather than being friends with their children, the Bible instructs parents to, *"Discipline your son, and he will give you peace; he will bring delight to your soul"* (Proverbs 29:17).

▶ The Sibling Relationship

When children live in a home where they feel they must compete for a finite amount of acceptance, approval, and attention from their parents, they become jealous and envious of one another. In this spirit of competition and mistrust, it is difficult for them to form friendships with one another. As competitors, they ...

- *Create* ways to undermine each other's successes
- *Coerce* each other into doing wrongful deeds
- *Criticize* one another often and in public

In essence, they have difficulty even speaking a kind word to one another.

"Israel loved Joseph more than any of his other sons, because he had been born to him in his old age; and he made a richly ornamented robe for him. When his brothers saw that their father loved him more than any of them, they hated him and could not speak a kind word to him" (Genesis 37:3–4).

CAUSES OF FAILED FRIENDSHIPS

They just can't keep their mouths shut.

For seven days and seven nights they commiserate in silence with their traumatized friend who has had his property, children, and health taken away from him by Satan. Job is a blameless man who is undergoing a fiery test of faith. The adversary said Job would fail the test and curse God to His face, but will he?

The suffering servant and his three friends have no idea about the showdown in the heavenlies, so the trio mulls over Job's plight. On the eighth day, they begin touting the following diagnosis: Job isn't blameless, he's bad. Job's no saint, he's a sinner. Why else would he be suffering so?

And the remedy from his presumptuous pals? *Repentance!* How quickly one "friend" spouts off his pious opinion.

> "We have examined this, and it is true.
> So hear it and apply it to yourself."
> (Job 5:27)

> "Your sin prompts your mouth;
> you adopt the tongue of the crafty.
> Your own mouth condemns you, not mine;
> your own lips testify against you."
> (Job 15:5–6)

The two other attackers speak up. Before long the three men are verbally blasting poor Job with presumptions of sin and guilt. They are swirling in a sea of self-pride, self-defensiveness, and self-righteousness, convinced their counsel will straighten up crooked Job.

"Is not your wickedness great? Are not your sins endless?" the ringleader tragically questions and then blasts Job with a series of false accusations. *"That is why snares are all around you, why sudden peril terrifies you"* (Job 22:5, 10).

As Job tries to defend himself, the second sniper launches a verbal assault: *"Your words are a blustering wind. Does God pervert justice? Does the Almighty pervert what is right? When your children sinned against him, he gave them over to the penalty of their sin"* (Job 8:2–4). So not only is Job a horrible sinner, so were his ten children who died! Talk about piling on the pain!

And from the lips of the third assailant: *"Is this talker to be vindicated? ... I hear a rebuke that dishonors me, and my understanding inspires me to reply. ... The mirth of the wicked is brief, the joy of the godless lasts but a moment. Though his pride reaches to the heavens and his head touches the clouds, he will perish forever, like his own dung"* (Job 11:2; 20:3, 5–7).

What happened to encouragement and compassion?

Those qualities were blatantly absent. Being self-focused or self-absorbed will send a friendship down the slippery slope of self-destruction as fast as anything. Friendship requires selflessness and a focus on others.

SELF-FOCUSED SABOTAGE

Do you have a "friend" in your life who fails to be a real friend? One who is ...

▶ **Self-centered**: absorbed with personal needs and desires?[13]

▶ **Self-conscious**: shy, uncomfortable with attention from others?[14]

▶ **Self-deceiving**: not honest about facts and feelings?

▶ **Self-defensive**: always justifying actions?

▶ **Self-pitying**: focusing on personal sorrow?

▶ **Self-prideful**: perfectionistic?[15]

▶ **Self-righteous**: judgmental?[16]

▶ **Self-serving**: controlling and manipulative?[17]

▶ **Self-sufficient**: not making quality time to nurture friendships?[18]

Relationships in which self is the focus demonstrate the truth of Isaiah's words:

> "We all, like sheep, have gone astray,
> each of us has turned to his own way;
> and the LORD has laid on him the iniquity
> of us all." (Isaiah 53:6)

New Friendships Shouldn't Be a Threat to Old Friends

QUESTION: "How can I reassure one of my dearest friends that my new friend is not a threat to our friendship?"

ANSWER: One of the best ways of explaining the special place each friend occupies in your life is to compare your heart to a large house and compare your friends to rooms in your house. Each room is different and special in its own way and is used for situations suitable for its design. For example, the sitting room is used for sitting and visiting with special people while the game room is used for playing games and having fun.

Each room has its own décor and atmosphere, and serves a necessary purpose within the house. Just as the kitchen cannot replace the bedroom, the living room cannot replace the laundry room.

To take this illustration further, within your "house." For example ...

- The entry way is cheerful and bright, friendly and inviting, and may remind you of "Sue."

- The living room is formal and somewhat inhibiting with elegant furnishings, perhaps reminding you of "Carlos."

- The dining room is less formal with large windows and colorful floral arrangements, and may make you think of "Jayla."

- The kitchen is always full of good food and smells of freshly brewed coffee, which may bring "Kerry" to mind.
- The family room is warm and spacious with comfortable sofas and chairs for relaxing, making you perhaps think of "Maria."
- The bedroom is roomy but cozy and comfortable with down pillows and a soft mattress, perhaps a perfect picture of "Angela."
- The laundry room is the messy room in the house with clothes in piles waiting to be washed and cleaning products on the countertops, perhaps like "Laura."

So you see, one friend cannot be replaced by another friend because each friend is one-of-a-kind and is used by God to meet your needs in unique ways like no one else can.

"From him the whole body, joined and held together by every supporting ligament, grows and builds itself up in love, as each part does its work" (Eph. 4:16).

WHY DO Friends Fall into Manipulation?

Failing to trust God to give us lasting love and loyalty, failing to depend on God to give us significance and security, and failing to look to God to give us fulfillment and contentment leaves us to our own devices—our own resources. The result is that many of us turn to coercive, deceptive, and cunning tactics to control others, our plans, and our schemes. In short, we turn to manipulation. But this is what God says: *"Cursed is the one who trusts in man, who depends on flesh for his strength and whose heart turns away from the Lord. ... But blessed is the man who trusts in the Lord, whose confidence is in him."* (Jeremiah 17:5, 7)

And what about those who allow themselves to be coerced, pressured, or deceived, rather than Spirit led? Rather than trusting in God, they trust in others. So the manipulators lead and the manipulated follow, because they have ...

▶ Misjudged Priorities[19]

- "What others think of me and how they feel about me is more important than anything."
- "The wishes and desires of others take precedence over my own."
- "I am willing to do whatever it takes to please the significant people in my life, even if it means violating my conscience."

But the Bible says, *"Stop trusting in man, who has but a breath in his nostrils. Of what account is he?"* (Isaiah 2:22).

▶ Misdirected Fear

- "I can't afford to say or do anything that might make a friend angry at me."
- "Just the thought of being rejected by a friend fills me with fear."
- "I am not about to go against a friend whose

approval I need because I fear losing the friendship."

But the Bible says, *"Do not fear the reproach of men or be terrified by their insults. For the moth will eat them up like a garment; the worm will devour them like wool. But my righteousness will last forever, my salvation through all generations"* (Isaiah 51:7–8).

▶ Misguided Acceptance

- "My acceptance by friends is based solely on what I do for them or how well I perform around them."
- "My value is dependent on how acceptable I am and on the acceptability of my work."
- "My worth is determined by the degree to which I am able to please my friends and do what they expect of me."

But the Bible says, *"The very hairs of your head are all numbered. Don't be afraid; you are worth more than many sparrows"* (Luke 12:7).

▶ Misunderstood Friendships

- "I know my friendships aren't perfect, but they meet my needs. They can't be that unhealthy."
- "As long as my friendships work for me, I see no need to scrutinize them to see if they are truly healthy or not."
- "What is there to understand about my friendships as long as they provide me with companionship?"

But the Bible says, *"He who gets wisdom loves his own soul; he who cherishes understanding prospers"* (Proverbs 19:8).

▶ Misplaced Dependencies

- "My friends give my life meaning and purpose. I would not want to live without them, and I could not live without their support."

- "I depend on my friends to make me feel loved, significant, and secure—without them I would be lost and alone."

- "I must have the acceptance and approval of my friends to feel good about myself."

But the Bible says, *"We speak as men approved by God to be entrusted with the gospel. We are not trying to please men but God, who tests our hearts"* (1 Thessalonians 2:4).

▶ Mistaken Identity

- "My world revolves around my friends, their hopes and dreams, their thoughts and actions."

- "My friends define who I am, and their treatment of me determines my worth."

- "I wouldn't think of doing anything or going anywhere on my own without my friends— my life is too wrapped up in their lives."

But the Bible says, *"The LORD is your life"* (Deuteronomy 30:20).

When Adam and Eve chose to distrust God as their faithful friend and disobey God as their sovereign Lord, they ended up being ashamed of their nakedness—ashamed of themselves. So they covered up their bodies and hid from God, the One who lovingly created them and who loved them perfectly.

Even today—as their offspring—we put on our own version of fig leaves to cover ourselves from being seen as we perceive ourselves to be. We fear personal exposure and so we hide from those whose friendship we desire and whom we desire to befriend. But our hiding doesn't stop there. We also hide from God, who is our best friend. And we even hide from ourselves! Our actions testify to the truth that *"Everyone who does evil hates the light, and will not come into the light for fear that his deeds will be exposed."* (John 3:20)

The most common barriers to intimacy within friendships include ...

▶ **Fear of being vulnerable**

- Anticipating the loss of love and respect
- Anticipating the loss of independence and individuality
- Anticipating the loss of control and self-determination

"In his heart a man plans his course, but the LORD determines his steps" (Proverbs 16:9).

▶ Fear of personal disclosure

- Expecting disapproval because of past failures
- Expecting disapproval because of present weaknesses
- Expecting disapproval because of the "real me"

"I sought the LORD, and he answered me; he delivered me from all my fears" (Psalm 34:4).

▶ Fear of taking risks

- Focusing on negative messages from parents who withheld nurturing and encouragement
- Focusing on negative behavior of significant others who were critical and condemning
- Focusing on negative personal behavior that produces shame, separation, isolation, and less transparency

"In God I trust; I will not be afraid. What can mortal man do to me?" (Psalm 56:4).

▶ Fear of repeated rejection

- Remembering past rejection from family members
- Remembering rejection in a significant love relationship
- Remembering past rejection of self

"Forget the former things; do not dwell on the past" (Isaiah 43:18).

Job reels from the relentless assaults, labeling his accusatory friends as *"miserable comforters."* *"How long will you torment me and crush me with words?"* Job actually acknowledges, *"Ten times now you have reproached me; shamelessly you attack me"* (Job 16:2; 19:2–3).

In spite of Job's inability to comprehend all of his painful losses, he still put his full reliance on the Lord, saying, *"I know that my Redeemer lives, and that in the end he will stand upon the earth. And after my skin has been destroyed, yet in my flesh I will see God; I myself will see him with my own eyes—I, and not another. How my heart yearns within me!"* (Job 19:25–27).

Eventually the tormenting does come to an end and the trio is finally humbled. God Himself speaks up and brands the counsel of all three men as *foolish.* Those who presumed to speak for God are now silenced by Him. God directs a statement to the most vocal victimizer: *"I am angry with you and your two friends, because you have not spoken of me what is right, as my servant Job has"* (Job 42:7).

Ultimately Job is vindicated and *"the LORD blessed the latter part of Job's life more than the first"* (Job 42:12). And more so, in spite of his faithless friends, he learned to rely on the Lord to be his security. He found his Redeemer to be his Foundation and his faithful Friend.

► **WRONG BELIEFS:**

"I wish I had a friend who made me feel wanted, someone who gave me a sense of significance.[20] I need a friend who will give me unconditional love without wanting to change me. My life would be complete with such a friend."

► **RIGHT BELIEFS:**

"The Lord is the only Friend whose love is always unconditional and unchangeable. And because He loves me, He will change me from the inside out—and sometimes He will change me through the friends He gives me.

"Instead of focusing on *getting* friendship, I will focus on *giving* it. My joy and significance will be found in serving and befriending others as an extension of the Lord's love."[21]

"My command is this: Love each other as I have loved you" (John 15:12).

How Can I Have an Authentic Friendship with Christ?

There are four spiritual truths you need to know.

FOUR POINTS OF GOD'S PLAN

#1 God's Purpose for You is *Salvation*.

What was God's motive in sending Christ to earth?

To express His love for you by saving you! The Bible says, *"God so loved the world that he gave his one and only Son, that whoever believes in him shall not perish but have eternal life. For God did not send his Son into the world to condemn the world, but to save the world through him"* (John 3:16–17).

What was Jesus' purpose in coming to earth?

To forgive your sins, to empower you to have victory over sin, and to enable you to live a fulfilled life! Jesus said, *"I have come that they may have life, and have it to the full"* (John 10:10).

#2 Your Problem is *Sin*.

What exactly is sin?

Sin is living independently of God's standard— knowing what is right, but choosing what is wrong. The Bible says, *"Anyone, then, who knows the good he ought to do and doesn't do it, sins"* (James 4:17).

What is the major consequence of sin?

Spiritual "death"—eternal separation from God. Scripture states, *"Your iniquities* [sins] *have separated you from your God"* (Isaiah 59:2).

"For the wages of sin is death, but the gift of God is eternal life in Christ Jesus our Lord" (Romans 6:23).

#3 God's Provision for You is the *Savior*.

Can anything remove the penalty for sin?

Yes! Jesus died on the cross to personally pay the penalty for your sins.

"God demonstrates his own love for us in this: While we were still sinners, Christ died for us" (Romans 5:8).

What can keep you from being separated from God?

Belief in (entrusting your life to) Jesus Christ as the only way to God the Father. Jesus says, *"I am the way and the truth and the life. No one comes to the Father except through me"* (John 14:6).

#4 Your Part is *Surrender.*

Give Christ control of your life—entrusting yourself to Him.

"Jesus said to his disciples, 'If anyone would come after me, he must deny himself and take up his cross [die to your own self-rule] and follow me. For whoever wants to save his life will lose it, but whoever loses his life for me will find it. What good will it be for a man if he gains the whole world, yet forfeits his soul?'" (Matthew 16:24–26).

Place your faith in (rely on) Jesus Christ as your personal Lord and Savior and reject your "good works" as a means of earning God's approval.

"It is by grace you have been saved, through faith—and this not from yourselves, it is the gift of God—not by works, so that no one can boast" (Ephesians 2:8–9).

The moment you choose to receive Jesus as your Lord and Savior—entrusting your life to Him—He comes to live inside you. Then He gives you His power to live the fulfilled life God has planned for you. If you want to be fully forgiven by God, to enter into a covenant friendship with Him, and become the person God created you to be, you can tell Him in a simple, heartfelt prayer like this:

PRAYER OF SALVATION

*"God, I want a real relationship with You—
a forever friendship with You.
I admit that many times I've chosen to go
my own way instead of Your way.
Please forgive me for my sins.
Jesus, thank You for dying on the cross
to pay the penalty for my sins.
Come into my life to be my Lord, my
Savior, and my Friend.
Change me from the inside out and make
me the person You created me to be.
In Your holy name I pray. Amen."*

What Can You Expect Now?

If you sincerely prayed this prayer, look at what God says! *"His divine power has given us everything we need for life and godliness through our knowledge of him who called us by his own glory and goodness. Through these he has given us his very great and precious promises, so that through them you may participate in the divine nature and escape the corruption in the world caused by evil desires"* (2 Peter 1:3–4).

STEPS TO SOLUTION

It could be so easy to neglect, even forget. After all, David is now King of Israel, and he is immersed in the matters of a monarch. His days are filled with ruling, judging, and safeguarding the people who have been entrusted to him. That promise made seemingly so long ago could easily be broken. The one to whom it was made is dead, David will never see him in the flesh again.

But David is faithful and determined not to forget his friendship covenant with Jonathan, but rather to honor it. And so he inquires, *"Is there anyone still left of the house of Saul to whom I can show kindness for Jonathan's sake?"* (2 Samuel 9:1).

A servant tells David about a son of Jonathan who is crippled. Mephibosheth is brought before the king and becomes the recipient of glorious covenant blessings. *"'Don't be afraid,' David said to him, 'for I will surely show you kindness for the sake of your father Jonathan. I will restore to you all the land that belonged to your grandfather Saul, and you will always eat at my table'"* (2 Samuel 9:7).

KEY VERSE TO MEMORIZE

"A friend loves at all times, and a brother is born for adversity."
(Proverbs 17:17)

Key Passage to Read

Realize how extraordinary this is: If you have given your life to Christ, He has made you His friend and He has become your Friend. You share a very special friendship, but not in a way that many understand, for your friendship is based on *covenant*. You have become one with Christ, and as a result of this covenant friendship, you are bonded to other believers and are to befriend those who are in spiritual covenant with Him.

Philippians 2:1–8

The Heart of Harmony

▶ *"If you have any encouragement from being united with Christ, if any comfort from his love, if any fellowship with the Spirit, if any tenderness and compassion, then make my joy complete by being like-minded, having the same love, being one in spirit and purpose."*

The Danger of Disharmony

▶ *"Do nothing out of selfish ambition or vain conceit, but in humility consider others better than yourselves. Each of you should look not only to your own interests, but also to the interests of others. Your attitude should be the same as that of Christ Jesus: Who, being in very nature God, did not consider equality with God something to be grasped, but made himself nothing, taking the very nature of a servant, being made in human likeness. And being found in appearance as a man, he humbled himself and became obedient to death—even death on a cross!"*

Spiritually united friends have special unity. We all want to feel connected with those we care about.

If you are spiritually united with Christ, you will have a spiritual unity with other Christians.

In following Christ's example as a covenant friend, you are to relate to each other as He relates to you. Therefore you are to ...

▶ **Find** encouragement from being friends. (v. 1)

▶ **Comfort** one another with Christ's love. (v. 1)

▶ **Enjoy** Christian fellowship together. (v. 1)

▶ **Show** the tenderness and compassion of Christ to each other. (v. 1)

▶ **Be like-minded**. (v. 2)

▶ **Share** the love of Christ. (v. 2)

▶ **Be one in spirit** and purpose. (v. 2)

▶ **Do nothing** out of selfish ambition or vain conceit. (v. 3)

▶ **Humbly consider** others better than yourself. (v. 3)

▶ **Attend** not only to your personal interests but to other's interests. (v. 4)

▶ **Have the same attitude** toward one another as Christ has toward you. (v. 5)

▶ **Make self nothing**. (v. 7)

▶ **Take** the nature of a servant. (v. 7)

▶ **Humble** yourselves. (v. 8)

▶ **Be willing** to die for one another. (v. 8)

If you are in need of meaningful relationships through which God can multiply your enjoyment of life and through which He can work in your life to transform you more and more into the likeness of Christ, there are some tips that can help you begin the process of forming friendships.

> **"And we, who with unveiled faces all reflect the Lord's glory, are being transformed into his likeness with ever-increasing glory, which comes from the Lord, who is the Spirit." (2 Corinthians 3:18)**

As you step out in faith to find the people and establish the friendships God has planned specifically for you...

▶ **Don't put God in a box** or do the same to the people you meet by limiting your search to individuals who appear to have time on their hands.

- Busyness is not an "off limits" sign.
- Sometimes busy people are the best candidates for friendships.
- If God is the designer of a relationship, busyness will not be a problem, but a blessing.

  "Surely you remember, brothers, our toil and hardship; we worked night and day in order not to be a burden to anyone while we preached the gospel of God to you" (1 Thessalonians 2:9).

"Greet Mary, who worked very hard for you. ... Greet Tryphena and Tryphosa, those women who work hard in the Lord. Greet my dear friend Persis, another woman who has worked very hard in the Lord" (Romans 16:6, 12).

▶ **Look for opportunities** to meet other people who share your same values and interests.

- Join a small Bible study, Sunday School class, or book club.

- Attend neighborhood block parties or other local social events.

- Mix with people at work, at sporting events, or at the local gym or exercise club.

  "Make the most of every opportunity" (Colossians 4:5).

▶ **Be friendly and sociable** by smiling, introducing yourself to people in close proximity to you, and by inviting people to your home for social events.

- Make "small talk" about newsworthy events, the weather, or local sports team. Ask questions and then listen to the answers.

- Don't be offended or hurt if some people are unwilling to engage in conversation with you. It is not a negative reflection on you if another person is not in a good frame of mind for making light conversation.

- Invite someone you work with to have lunch with you one day just to "shoot the breeze" and get to know one another's likes and dislikes, interests and after-hours fun activities.

"Offer hospitality to one another without grumbling. Each one should use whatever gift he has received to serve others, faithfully administering God's grace in its various forms. If anyone speaks, he should do it as one speaking the very words of God. If anyone serves, he should do it with the strength God provides" (1 Peter 4:9–11).

"Do not forget to entertain strangers, for by so doing some people have entertained angels without knowing it" (Hebrews 13:2).

▶ **Relax and just be yourself**. Trust God to make you a person of interest to whomever would be a positive person in your life.

- Don't try to be the life of the party or play any role that doesn't come naturally to you.

- Be transparent by being natural, and not trying to impress anyone. You want a friend, not an audience, to applaud your abilities.

- Go with the flow by being spontaneous and flexible.

  "Do not think of yourself more highly than you ought" (Romans 12:3).

▶ **Eliminate expectations** of any kind and make it your goal to develop some skills that will help you engage in conversation when around new people.

- Do not expect to "connect" on a deep level with someone at a first meeting when so little is known about one another.

- Be content to just meet some new people and learn something about them that might broaden your perspective or pique your interest.

- Trust God to use your efforts for His purposes in your life. Be thankful for the privilege of meeting and spending time with people He cherishes and created for His particular purposes.

"So in everything, do to others what you would have them do to you, for this sums up the Law and the Prophets" (Matthew 7:12).

HOW TO Reach Out and Be a Friend

One of the best antidotes for loneliness is helping others—moving your focus from trying to meet your own needs to trying to help meet the needs of others. Ask God to help you joyfully and faithfully support those He brings into your life in need of help and encouragement.

To initiate relationships, generously plant seeds of friendship into the lives of others. When you sow seeds of kindness and friendship in the lives of others, you will eventually reap the rewards of kindness and friendship in your own life. Simple acts of kindness can go a long way. A warm smile, a kind word, an invitation to lunch, all communicate love and concern.

"Do not be deceived: God cannot be mocked. A man reaps what he sows" (Galatians 6:7).

▶ **Understand the pain of others.**

- Imagine how you would feel if you were in the other person's situation.
- Look for practical ways to help.
- Don't be critical.
- Acknowledge that it is by the grace of God you are not in a similar situation.
- Be a good listener.

Imitate the compassion of Paul toward Timothy: *"Recalling your tears, I long to see you, so that I may be filled with joy"* (2 Timothy 1:4).

▶ **Look for ways to express love to others.**

- Offer help to someone in need (shop for groceries, prepare a meal, carpool, etc.).
- Send an encouraging card or note to someone.
- Help someone complete a task.
- Give someone a small gift (flowers, cookies, bookmark, etc.) communicating God's love.
- Perform random acts of kindness without expecting anything in return.

Remember the words of the apostle John: *"Dear friends, let us love one another, for love comes from God"* (1 John 4:7).

▶ **Don't demand change.**

- Be flexible.
- Give others time to grow.
- Pray for them.
- Have a heart of love and acceptance toward others.
- Make every attempt for peace.
- Don't require perfection from yourself or others.

Heed the wisdom of King Solomon: *"The wise in heart are called discerning, and pleasant words promote instruction"* (Proverbs 16:21).

▶ **Decide to diversify your activities and goals.**

- Give others the opportunity to know you.
- Be open to change.
- Participate in new and different activities.
- Be willing to give up old activities that are no longer useful or edifying.
- Pray for God's direction in choosing your activities.

Always praise God in your heart: *"Sing to him a new song; play skillfully, and shout for joy"* (Psalm 33:3).

▶ **Initiate invitations** (calls, visits).

- Write letters to out-of-town friends and relatives.
- Invite people to have lunch or dinner with you.

- Invite people to your home.
- Offer your home for meetings and social gatherings.
- Join a committee in your church welcoming visitors and new members.
- Initiate calls to people, asking them how they are doing.

Always put into practice the words of Jesus: *"Then Jesus said to his host, 'When you give a luncheon or dinner, do not invite your friends, your brothers or relatives, or your rich neighbors; if you do, they may invite you back and so you will be repaid. But when you give a banquet, invite the poor, the crippled, the lame, the blind, and you will be blessed. Although they cannot repay you, you will be repaid at the resurrection of the righteous'"* (Luke 14:12–14).

▶ **Think Positive Thoughts.**

- "I am a typical human being with the same feelings, desires, and needs as anyone else."
- "I have worth and value even if some people don't like me."
- "It's okay for me to express my thoughts and feelings even if no one else shares them."
- "No one likes being rejected, but everyone experiences it at one time or another."
- "Just because I don't like someone's behavior doesn't mean the person has no value."
- "Life is unfair and people are sinners, but I can love and pray for them."

As Jesus commanded, *"Love your enemies and pray for those who persecute you"* (Matthew 5:44).

▶ **Be rid of bitterness.**

- Pray for your enemies and those who have hurt you.
- Focus on the blessings in your life.
- Trust your choices to God. He is sovereign.
- Allow God to handle your hurts and disappointments.
- Bless others and leave vengeance to God.
- Forgive others and give them the same grace God gives you.

Be sure to obey the command of God: *"See to it that no one misses the grace of God and that no bitter root grows up to cause trouble and defile many"* (Hebrews 12:15).

HOW TO Fan the Flame of Friendship

David proceeds to give back to Mephibosheth all the land that once belonged to his grandfather Saul. He also is given a lifetime invitation to eat at the king's table.

As David is ready to bestow more blessings, Mephibosheth interjects a question. With head bowed down, he asks, *"What is your servant, that you should notice a dead dog like me?"* (2 Samuel 9:8). David never answers him, but conveys Mephibosheth's value and worth in David's eyes through further blessing.

The servant who tells David about Mephibosheth is instructed that he, his sons, and his servants are to provide for him by farming the land and harvesting the crops. He obeys the word of the king and Mephibosheth's life is forever changed because of David's faithfulness to his friendship covenant. The Bible records David's compassionate "open door policy" to Jonathan's crippled son. *"Mephibosheth lived in Jerusalem, because he always ate at the king's table, and he was crippled in both feet"* (2 Samuel 9:13).

As you seek to fan the flame of friendship, there are some helpful Do's and Don'ts you will want to heed and apply.

Do's

▶ *Do* recognize that you need wise friends.[22]

"He who walks with the wise grows wise, but a companion of fools suffers harm" (Proverbs 13:20).

▶ *Do* look for others in need of a friend.[23]

"Each of you should look not only to your own interests, but also to the interests of others" (Philippians 2:4).

▶ *Do* ask God to bring a faithful friend into your life.

"If we ask anything according to his will, he hears us" (1 John 5:14).

▶ **Do** be approachable by smiling at others and looking them in the eye.[24]

"A happy heart makes the face cheerful, but heartache crushes the spirit" (Proverbs 15:13).

▶ **Do** speak to others by name.

"The watchman opens the gate for him, and the sheep listen to his voice. He calls his own sheep by name and leads them out" (John 10:3).

▶ **Do** listen attentively to others.[25]

There is *"a time to be silent and a time to speak"* (Ecclesiastes 3:7).

▶ **Do** give genuine compliments and encouragement.[26]

"Pleasant words are a honeycomb, sweet to the soul and healing to the bones" (Proverbs 16:24).

▶ **Do** ask open-ended questions.[27]

- "What do you like most about your job?"
- "Who has been the best influence in your life?"
- "What would you change about your childhood?"

"The purposes of a man's heart are deep waters, but a man of understanding draws them out" (Proverbs 20:5).

▶ **Do** encourage others to verbalize their feelings.

- "I sense that you are hurting."
- "Has something difficult happened in your life?"
- "How do you feel about what has happened?"
- "I want you to know that I care."

"A wise man's heart guides his mouth, and his lips promote instruction" (Proverbs 16:23).

▶ **Do** look for the kernel of truth in your friend's criticism.

"As iron sharpens iron, so one man sharpens another" (Proverbs 27:17).

> *"You can make more friends in two months by becoming interested in other people than you can in two years by trying to get other people interested in you."* [28]
> —Dale Carnegie

DON'TS

▶ **Don't** wait for others to reach out to you; take the first step.[29]

"God did not give us a spirit of timidity, but a spirit of power, of love and of self-discipline" (2 Timothy 1:7).

▶ ***Don't*** share just facts; share your true feelings.[30]

- "Recently, I have had trouble with feelings of discouragement."

"Surely you desire truth in the inner parts; you teach me wisdom in the inmost place" (Psalm 51:6).

▶ ***Don't*** expect everyone to like you.[31]

"If the world hates you, keep in mind that it hated me first" (John 15:18).

▶ ***Don't*** expect your friends' friends to be your friends.

"My God will meet all your needs according to his glorious riches in Christ Jesus" (Philippians 4:19).

▶ ***Don't*** focus on your interests; ask about the interests of others.[32]

"Do nothing out of selfish ambition or vain conceit, but in humility consider others better than yourselves" (Philippians 2:3).

▶ ***Don't*** be too quick to voice your own opinions.[33]

"A fool finds no pleasure in understanding but delights in airing his own opinions" (Proverbs 18:2).

▶ ***Don't*** harbor unforgiveness over offenses.[34]

"Be kind and compassionate to one another, forgiving each other, just as in Christ God forgave you" (Ephesians 4:32).

▶ ***Don't*** share negative information about others.[35]

"A perverse man stirs up dissension, and a gossip separates close friends" (Proverbs 16:28).

▶ ***Don't*** look to a friend to meet your needs for love, significance, and security, but look to God.[36]

"Your love, O LORD, reaches to the heavens, your faithfulness to the skies. Your righteousness is like the mighty mountains, your justice like the great deep. O LORD, you preserve both man and beast. How priceless is your unfailing love! Both high and low among men find take refuge in the shadow of your wings" (Psalm 36:5–7).

▶ ***Don't*** let your friend take the place that God alone should have.[37]

"You shall have no other gods before me" (Exodus 20:3).

HOW TO Listen and Liberate a Friend

Everyone likes to be heard, to be understood, *to matter!* And everyone has probably heard the saying, "God gave us one mouth and two ears so we would listen twice as much as we speak." Unfortunately, while everyone wants to be heard, not everyone wants to hear, to listen, or to understand. Maybe that is one reason Jesus gave us what has come to be known as the Golden Rule: *"Do to others as you would have them do to you"* (Luke 6:31).

If you want to be heard, learn to listen first. Then you may earn the right to be heard.

> "My dear brothers, take note of this:
> Everyone should be quick to listen,
> slow to speak and slow to become angry."
> (James 1:19)

If you want to be an effective listener, you must possess a heart that yearns to ...

▶ **Put** others before self

▶ **Meet** the needs of others

▶ **Gain** understanding of others more than agreement with others

▶ **Be** Christlike toward others

Let righteous Job be your example:

> "I waited while you spoke, I listened to your
> reasoning; while you were searching for
> words, I gave you my full attention."
> (Job 32:11–12)

If you want to be an effective listener, you must ...

▶ **Look** into the eyes of the person speaking to you.

▶ **Maintain** physical closeness.

▶ **Lean** toward the person.

▶ **Keep** your body in a relaxed position.

▶ **Face** the person squarely.

▶ **Express** attentiveness and concern through your eyes and facial expressions.

▶ **Allow** for periods of silence to give the person time to think.

▶ **Clarify** what is being said by repeating to the person what has been said to you:

"What I heard you say is _____. Is that correct? Did I miss anything?"

▶ **Reflect** back to the speaker the feelings expressed or perceived behind what they have shared:

"You appear to be feeling quite _____ toward _____ for _____."

▶ **Hypothesize** what the person's feelings, ideas, or desires might logically be when they have not been clearly stated or perceived:

"I can see that you might have felt _____ considering the circumstances. I can imagine that you thought _____ and wanted to _____."

▶ **Ask** open-ended questions that will provide more information or clear up any confusion rather than questions that can be answered with *yes* or *no*:

"Could you elaborate on that for me? How did it make you feel?"

▶ **Offer** encouraging statements or questions that communicate warmth and caring:

"Please continue. I want to know what happened

to you and the impact it had on you." "Right, I understand." "Hmmm." "You mean that really happened? He actually _____?" "How terrible that must have been for you."

▶ **Provide** a brief summary of what has been said including experiences, feelings, goals, etc.:

"If I've understood correctly, you _____ and you felt _____ and you want _____. Am I correct?"

HOW TO Move toward Intimacy

Begin nurturing intimate friendships by taking the responsibility to develop positive relational patterns. You can do this by taking three steps:

1. *Change* your focus from the displeasing traits in the personalities of others to the positive traits they possess.

2. *Ask* God to reveal the deficiencies that reside in your own heart.

3. *Submit* to the Holy Spirit's prompting toward loving interaction with others.

Intimacy is based on truth and wisdom, two qualities that God desires us to possess and demonstrate in our friendships.

"Surely you desire truth in the inner parts; you teach me wisdom in the inmost place."
(Psalm 51:6)

The Bible gives clear guidelines for developing positive, loving patterns of relating to others in a way that will promote intimate, lifelong forever friendships.

▶ **Agreement**—Choose a relationship with someone who has the same basic beliefs and values as you do.

"Do not be yoked together with unbelievers. For what do righteousness and wickedness have in common? Or what fellowship can light have with darkness? What harmony is there between Christ and Belial? What does a believer have in common with an unbeliever?" (2 Corinthians 6:14–15).

▶ **Commitment**—Pledge to maintain the relationship as an act of the will.

"Jonathan made a covenant with David because he loved him as himself. Jonathan took off the robe he was wearing and gave it to David, along with his tunic, and even his sword, his bow and his belt" (1 Samuel 18:3–4).

▶ **Encouragement**—Compliment and build others up.

"Each of us should please his neighbor for his good, to build him up" (Romans 15:2).

▶ **Faithfulness**—Maintain lasting loyalty.

"Let love and faithfulness never leave you; bind them around your neck, write them on the tablet of your heart" (Proverbs 3:3).

▶ **Forgiveness**—Give up personal rights and release hurts and offenses to God.

"Bear with each other and forgive whatever grievances you may have against one another. Forgive as the Lord forgave you" (Colossians 3:13).

▶ **Gentleness**—Use kind, tender words and actions.

"A gentle answer turns away wrath, but a harsh word stirs up anger" (Proverbs 15:1).

▶ **Honesty**—Communicate truthfully with a commitment to mutual correction for the sake of developing Christlike character.

"Wounds from a friend can be trusted, but an enemy multiplies kisses" (Proverbs 27:6).

▶ **Humility**—Know your own faults and weaknesses.

"Slander no one, to be peaceable and considerate, and to show true humility toward all men. At one time we too were foolish, disobedient, deceived and enslaved by all kinds of passions and pleasures. We lived in malice and envy, being hated and hating one another. But when the kindness and love of God our Savior appeared, he saved us, not because of righteous things we had done, but because of his mercy" (Titus 3:2–5).

▶ **Love**—Take the most constructive, redemptive, and edifying action possible on behalf of another.

"This is how we know what love is: Jesus Christ

laid down his life for us. And we ought to lay down our lives for our brothers" (1 John 3:16).

▶ **Patience**—Be slow to anger.

"A patient man has great understanding, but a quick-tempered man displays folly" (Proverbs 14:29).

▶ **Respect**—Honor others above yourself.

"Be devoted to one another in brotherly love. Honor one another above yourselves" (Romans 12:10).

▶ **Spiritual Maturity**—Grow up in your personal relationship with the Lord.

"The fear of the Lord is the beginning of wisdom, and knowledge of the Holy One is understanding" (Proverbs 9:10).

HOW TO Commit to Intimacy in Friendship

Deeper levels of friendship are generally developed over time after trust has been tested and established as solid and enduring. Once a foundation of trust has been laid, intimacy can safely occur between two friends who have chosen to be committed to one another for life.

"But show me unfailing kindness like that of the Lord as long as I live, so that I may not be killed, and do not ever cut off your kindness from my family—not even when the Lord has cut off every

one of David's enemies from the face of the earth."
(1 Samuel 20:14–15)

Intimacy in friendship is attained through acts of the will ...

▶ **I will love** you unconditionally.

▶ **I will not reject** you.

▶ **I will keep** my heart vulnerable to you.

▶ **I will not blame** you for the way I feel.

▶ **I will make** it safe for you to be honest with me.

▶ **I will not use** anything you say against you.

▶ **I will be willing** to reveal my inner fears and disappointments to you.

▶ **I will not interrupt** you when you share your thoughts and feelings.

▶ **I will share** my hopes and desires with you.

▶ **I will not try** to manipulate or control you.

▶ **I will consider** your point of view.

▶ **I will not be** defensive with you.

▶ **I will be accountable** to you.

▶ **I will not try** to force you to meet my expectations.

▶ **I will reach out** to you with affection.

▶ **I will not withdraw** from you emotionally or physically.

▶ **I will encourage** your spiritual growth.

▶ **I will not engage** in faultfinding with you.

▶ **I will view** conflict between us as an opportunity for growth.

▶ **I will not reject** that God is using you in my life.

"Be imitators of God, therefore, as dearly loved children and live a life of love, just as Christ loved us and gave himself up for us as a fragrant offering and sacrifice to God." (Ephesians 5:1–2)

HOW TO Communicate to Form and Further Friendships

What helps us form friendships and keep friendships growing and deepening? The simple answer is *communication*. Whether the friendship is peer to peer, younger to older, spouse to spouse, meaningful communication is vital when you are attempting to connect and move to deeper levels.

But "connecting communication" is not just any kind of speaking. Through the use of one single proverb, the Bible paints a picture of how we can communicate to broaden and deepen friendships.

"He who loves a pure heart and whose speech is gracious will have the king for his friend." (Proverbs 22:11)

There are productive and nonproductive ways to talk; correct ways that help you connect and incorrect ways that only build barriers. Therefore, remember these simple but significant rules:

SEVEN RULES OF RELATING IN FRIENDSHIP

▶ **Don't interrupt each other.** If your friend is talking, you are not to interrupt, but are to listen intently, always being courteous to one another.

▶ **Don't press for answers to probing questions.** If your friend says, "I'm not ready to answer that one yet." You can ask *once*, "Are you sure? I really would like to know." The goal is not to learn everything at one time but to begin meaningful dialogue that will foster intimacy between the two of you.

▶ **Don't say, "You shouldn't feel that way."** If your friend says, "I feel _____," you are *not* to communicate (through words, looks, or body language) your disapproval. Feelings are feelings. You can appropriately respond, "Is there something I can do to help you not feel this way?"

▶ **Don't project a prideful "I'm more open than you" attitude.** If your friend is uncomfortable (looking away, trying to change the subject, or actually wanting to leave the room), discreetly drop the conversation without developing a haughty attitude. Simply move on. Some things really can be too painful or personal to talk about—even in a close relationship.

▶ **Don't use slicing sarcasm.** If your friend does something you don't like, do not be sarcastic. Words can be weapons, and both teasing and sarcasm are too often the weapons of choice. They have a sharp double-edged point indicating the presence of cloaked anger. However, when sarcasm is reciprocal and used in a playful, humorous way with no malicious intent, it is acceptable and harmless.

▶ **Don't be oblivious to your nonverbal communication.** If you are feeling negative toward your friend, be aware of what you are communicating nonverbally. Facial expressions and body posturing often make negative, unhelpful statements. They may sometimes tell the truth, but words are clearer, more productive communicators.

▶ **Don't raise your voice.** If you feel irritated or angry, keep the volume of your voice at a level that is normally pleasant for you. Loudness does not encourage good communication and is a barrier to intimacy that's tough to break through. When upset, speak slow and low.

HOW TO Find Freedom from a Codependent Friendship

Codependency develops when a person is consumed by a drive to get personal, inner needs met through trying to be another person's "all-in-all." The road they travel is rocky and full of painful pitfalls because there is only one true Need-Meeter, and that is God. Fortunately, there is a "road to recovery" that is paved with peace, the peace that comes by *releasing* your desire to control or to change the person you love. When you give the Lord control of your life as well as the life of the person you love, you can rest in His assurance.

"My grace is sufficient for you,
for my power is made perfect in weakness."
(2 Corinthians 12:9)

RELEASE

Recognize that you are overly dependent on another person, then choose to place your dependency on God.

▶ **Admit** that your codependency is a sin.

▶ **Pray** that God will give you the desire to put Him first and to please Him in all of your friendships.

▶ **Realize** that God did not create you to meet all the needs of another person or to have all of your needs met by another person.

▶ **Determine** to look to the Lord to meet your needs and your friend's needs for love, significance, and security.[38]

"Love the Lord your God with all your heart and with all your soul and with all your mind and with all your strength" (Mark 12:30).

Examine your patterns of codependent thinking.

▶ **Don't believe** that pleasing people always pleases God.

▶ **Don't think** that you should be a "peace at any price" person.

▶ **Don't fear** losing the love of others when you refuse to rescue them from suffering the negative consequences of their own unwise choices.

▶ **Don't be pressured** into saying *yes* when you really believe you should say *no*.

"Each of you must put off falsehood and speak truthfully to his neighbor" (Ephesians 4:25).

Let Go of your "super-savior" mentality.

▶ **Confess** that you are trying to be God in the life of your friend.

▶ **Rely** on God to be actively working for good in the life of your loved one.

▶ **Realize** that you cannot *make* another person reliable, responsible, or righteous.

▶ **Rest** in God's sovereign control over all people, events, and circumstances.

"What you are doing is not good. You and these people who come to you will only wear yourselves out. The work is too heavy for you; you cannot handle it alone" (Exodus 18:17–18).

Extend forgiveness to those who have caused you pain.

▶ **Reflect** on any type of abuse you have experienced in the past—verbal, emotional, physical, spiritual, or sexual.

- What has been unjust and painful in your life?
- Whom do you need to forgive?
- Would you be willing to release this person and your pain to God?

"Be kind and compassionate to one another, forgiving each other, just as in Christ God forgave you" (Ephesians 4:32).

PRAYER OF FORGIVENESS

"God, You know the pain I experienced in my past. I don't want to keep carrying all this pain for the rest of my life.
I release (list hurts) into Your hands, and I ask You to heal my emotional pain.
Lord, You know what (name of person) has done to hurt me. As an act of my will, I choose to forgive (name).
I take (name) off of my emotional hook and put (name) onto Your emotional hook. Thank You, Lord Jesus, for setting me FREE.
In Your holy name I pray. Amen."

APPROPRIATE your identity **in Christ.**

▶ **Learn** to live out of your resources in Christ Jesus.

▶ **Know the truth**: "I can be emotionally set free because Christ lives in me."

"If the Son sets you free, you will be free indeed" (John 8:36).

▶ **Believe the truth**: "I can change from having my dependency on people to having my dependency on God through the power of Christ in me."

"Not that we are competent in ourselves to claim anything for ourselves, but our competence comes from God" (2 Corinthians 3:5).

▶ **Appropriate the truth**: "I will nurture only healthy, godly relationships because I belong to Christ."

"His divine power has given us everything we need for life and godliness through our knowledge of him who called us by his own glory and goodness. Through these he has given us his very great and precious promises, so that through them you may participate in the divine nature and escape the corruption in the world caused by evil desires" (2 Peter 1:3–4).

SET healthy boundaries.

▶ **Communicate** the necessity for change.

"I realize I have not been the kind of friend to you I should have been. I have depended on you far too much to meet my needs. And I have tried too hard to meet all of your needs. I have chosen to make a commitment to God and to myself to have only healthy friendships and to put God first in my life. I know I have responded in unhealthy ways to you, and I intend to begin responding in healthy ways by making decisions based on what is right in God's eyes."

▶ **Establish** what you need to ask forgiveness for.

"I realize I was wrong in _____ (not speaking up when I should have, not being the healthy, mature person I should have been in this relationship, etc.). Will you forgive me?"

▶ **Establish** what your limits of responsibility will be.

"I feel responsible for _____ (my own happiness). But I am not responsible for _____ (making you happy, making you feel significant, etc.). I want you to be happy, but I don't have the power to make you happy."

▶ **Establish** your limits of involvement.

"I want to _____ with/for you, but I don't feel led by God to _____ (be accountable to you for my time, to make my plans around your schedule, etc.)."

"The prudent see danger and take refuge, but the simple keep going and suffer for it" (Proverbs 27:12)

EXCHANGE your emotional focus for a spiritual focus.

▶ **Make** God and your spiritual growth your first priority.

▶ **Attend** an in-depth Bible study in order to know the heart of God and to grow spiritually with the people of God.

▶ **Memorize** sections of Scripture in order to put God's Word in your heart and to learn the ways of God.

▶ **Redirect** your thoughts to the Lord and take "prayer walks" (talking out loud to the Lord as you walk regularly in your neighborhood or on a trail).

"Direct me in the path of your commands, for there I find delight. Turn my heart toward your statutes and not toward selfish gain. Turn my eyes away from worthless things; preserve my life according to your word" (Psalm 119:35–37).

The cure for codependency is rooted in developing an ever-deepening relationship with the Lord. Your increased intimacy with Him will naturally conform you to His character. When you let the Lord live inside you and let His Word live in your heart, you can live in His power. This means that because Christ was not codependent *you will overcome codependency.*

"In this world you will have trouble.
But take heart! I have overcome the world."
(John 16:33)

RELEASING YOU

Releasing is not to stop loving you,
but is to love enough to stop leaning on you.

Releasing is not to stop caring for you,
but is to care enough to stop controlling you.

Releasing is not to turn away from you,
but is to turn to Christ, trusting His control
over you.

Releasing is not to harm you,
but is to realize "my help" has been harmful.

Releasing is not to hurt you,
but is to be willing to be hurt for healing.

Releasing is not to judge you,
but is to let the divine Judge judge me.

Releasing is not to restrict you,
but is to restrict my demands of you.

Releasing is not to refuse you,
but is to refuse to keep reality from you.

Releasing is not to cut myself off from you,
but is to prune the unfruitful away from you.

Releasing is not to prove my power over you,
but is to admit I am powerless to change
you.

Releasing is not to stop believing in you,
but is to believe the Lord alone will build
character in you.

Releasing you is not to condemn the past,
but is to cherish the present and commit our
future to God.

—June Hunt

Just as God established His creation with boundaries we call "laws," He made us in such a way that we, too, are to function with boundaries in our personal lives. They are not always easily set, but they are always essential to maintaining healthy friendships.

"Through Christ Jesus the law of the Spirit of life set me free from the law of sin and death." (Romans 8:2)

BOUNDARY

BUILD healthy boundaries.

▶ It's not too late to establish and practice new boundary patterns in your friendships.

▶ God loves you and wants you to have freedom-producing, life-protecting boundaries in your life.

"The highway of the upright avoids evil; he who guards his way guards his life" (Proverb 16:17).

OVERCOME others' disapproval.

▶ Seek God's approval over the approval of others and find your encouragement in Him.

▶ Personalize and memorize:

"The LORD *himself goes before* [me] *and will be with* [me]; *he will never leave* [me] *nor forsake* [me]. [I will] *not be afraid;* [I will] *not be discouraged"* (Deuteronomy 31:8).

U**PHOLD** biblical boundaries.

▶ God established boundaries for His entire creation from the very beginning.

▶ God has personal boundaries. He has set Himself apart, and there is none like Him.

*"I am the L*ORD *your God; consecrate yourselves and be holy, because I am holy"* (Leviticus 11:44).

N**OTIFY** others.

▶ Recognize and identify your resources and responsibilities to God, to friends, and to yourself.

▶ Communicate clearly newfound convictions regarding the need for boundaries in becoming more Christlike.

"Speaking the truth in love, we will in all things grow up into him who is the Head, that is, Christ" (Ephesians 4:15).

D**EVELOP** healthy friendships.

▶ As you establish healthier boundaries for yourself, you will want to be friends with people who also have set healthy boundaries for themselves.

▶ In living a life with boundaries, you will be more aware of boundary violations and avoid them— this is a sign you are getting healthier!

"Walk in the ways of good men and keep to the paths of the righteous" (Proverbs 2:20).

A**CCEPT** and extend forgiveness.

▶ Are there friends you need to forgive who have violated your boundaries?

▶ Are there friends you need to ask forgiveness from because you have trampled over their boundaries?

"Bear with each other and forgive whatever grievances you may have against one another. Forgive as the Lord forgave you" (Colossians 3:13).

R**EPAIR** broken boundaries.

▶ Commit in your heart to persist and to keep starting over until new healthy boundaries are firmly in place.

"Forget the former things; do not dwell on the past. See, I am doing a new thing! Now it springs up; do you not perceive it? I am making a way in the desert and streams in the wasteland" (Isaiah 43:18–19).

Y**IELD** and commit to healthy boundaries.

▶ Communicate your boundaries clearly and lovingly, and state what you will do if friends cross them.

▶ Follow through with your stated repercussions when your boundaries are crossed.

"My words come from an upright heart; my lips sincerely speak what I know" (Job 33:3).

Hesed is a Hebrew word used nearly 250 times in the Old Testament. It means "lovingkindness" and highlights love and loyalty, the two essential aspects of a covenant relationship.

When Jonathan requests that David show him *"unfailing kindness like that of the LORD as long as I live, so that I may not be killed, and do not ever cut off your kindness from my family"* (1 Samuel 20:14–15), it is *hesed* love that he is seeking from David.[40]

Covenants in the Old Testament were to be permanently binding and unchangeable. The parties involved carried out the terms of the covenant under the penalty of divine retribution should they try to avoid their obligations.

But in no way does David try to avoid the promises he made to his best friend, Jonathan. He beautifully expresses *hesed* love *"for Jonathan's sake"* (2 Samuel 9:1).

1 SAMUEL CHAPTERS 18–20; 23

Jonathan and David

▶ **Unity**—Jonathan became one in spirit with David. (18:1)

▶ **Sacrificial Love**—Jonathan loved David as he loved himself. (18:1)

▶ **Commitment**—Jonathan made a friendship covenant with David. (18:3)

▶ **Generosity**—Jonathan gave David his tunic, sword, bow, and belt. (18:4)

▶ **Honesty**—Jonathan warned David of his father's desire to kill him. (19:1–2)

▶ **Praise**—Jonathan spoke well of David to his father. (19:4)

▶ **Encouragement**—Jonathan told David not to fear for his life. (19:7)

▶ **Faithfulness**—Jonathan told David he would do whatever David wanted him to do. (20:4)

▶ **Trustworthiness**—Jonathan told David he could trust him to warn him. (20:9)

▶ **Loyalty**—Jonathan and David shared oaths to protect each other's families. (20:14–17)

▶ **Integrity**—Jonathan made the Lord witness to all he did for David. (20:42)

▶ **Compassion**—Jonathan was grieved at his father's treatment of David. (20:34)

▶ **Emotional vulnerability**—Jonathan and David kissed each other and wept together. (20:41)

▶ **Spiritual strengthening**—Jonathan encouraged David to lean on God for strength. (23:16)

▶ **Refusing rivalry**—Jonathan refused to compete with David for the throne, although he was the son of the king. (23:17)

"Oh, the comfort—the inexpressible comfort of feeling safe with a person— having neither to weigh thoughts nor measure words, but pouring them all right out, just as they are, chaff and grain together; certain that a faithful hand will take and sift them, keep what is worth keeping, and then with the breath of kindness blow the rest away." [41]
— Dinah Craik, *A Life for a Life*, 1859

One great failure in friendship is letting a friend lean on us for too long. The greatest gift we can give is fortifying our friend to lean on the Rock—our Redeemer— our only firm Foundation.
—June Hunt

SCRIPTURES TO MEMORIZE

Should I be totally trusting **in friendship** or **cautious**?

*"A righteous man is **cautious in friendship**, but the way of the wicked leads them astray."* (Proverbs 12:26)

Should I avoid becoming **friends** with those who are **easily angered**?

*"Do not make **friends** with a hot-tempered man, do not associate with one **easily angered**, or you may learn his ways and get yourself ensnared."* (Proverbs 22:24–25)

Why should I literally pray for **wise** friends in my daily **walk**?

*"He who **walks** with the **wise** grows wise, but a companion of fools suffers harm."* (Proverbs 13:20)

What value does the **earnest counsel** of a **friend** bring?

*"Perfume and incense **bring** joy to the heart, and the pleasantness of one's **friend** springs from his **earnest counsel**."* (Proverbs 27:9)

What does the Bible say about **one** who **falls down** and a **friend** who **can help him up**?

*"If **one falls down**, his **friend can help him up**. But pity the man who falls and has no one to help him up!"* (Ecclesiastes 4:10)

What is the **greatest love** a friend can show to **his friends**?

> "**Greater love** has no one than this, that he lay down his life for **his friends**." (John 15:13)

Can I get by with being **a friend** who **loves** only some **times**?

> "**A friend loves** at all **times**, and a brother is born for adversity." (Proverbs 17:17)

Why should I value the **wounds** of **a trusted friend**?

> "**Wounds** from **a friend** can be **trusted**, but an enemy multiplies kisses." (Proverbs 27:6)

NOTES

1. Jim Conway, *Making Real Friends in a Phony World* (Grand Rapids: Zondervan, 1989), 69.

2. James Strong, *Strong's Greek Lexicon*, (electronic edition; Online Bible Millennium Edition v. 1.13) ed. (Timnathserah Inc., July 6, 2002).

3. Robert Horst Balz and Gerhard Schneider, *Exegetical Dictionary of the New Testament*, vol. 3 (Grand Rapids: Eerdmans, 1993), 424.

4. Robert Horst Balz and Gerhard Schneider, *Exegetical Dictionary of the New Testament*, vol. 3 (Grand Rapids: Eerdmans, 1993), 425.

5. *Merriam-Webster Collegiate Dictionary*, s.v. "Friend," http://www.merriam-webster.com/dictionary/friend.

6. Gary Inrig, *Quality Friendship* (Chicago: Moody, 1981), 144-8.

7. W. E. Vine, Merrill F. Unger, William White, *Vine's Expository Dictionary of Biblical Words* (Nashville: Thomas Nelson, 1985), s.v. "Love."

8. Joe White and Mary White, *Friends & Friendship: The Secrets of Drawing Closer* (Colorado Springs, Colo.: NavPress, 1982), 33-8; Em Griffin, *Making Friends (& Making Them Count)* (Downers Grove, Ill.: InterVarsity, 1987), 141-2.

9. Lawrence J. Crabb, Jr., *Understanding People: Deep Longings for Relationship*, Ministry Resources Library (Grand Rapids: Zondervan, 1987), 15–16; Robert S. McGee, *The Search for Significance*, 2nd ed. (Houston, TX: Rapha, 1990), 27–30.

10. John Townsend, *Hiding from Love: How to Change the Withdrawal Patterns that Isolate and Imprison You* (Colorado Springs, CO: NavPress, 1991), 166.

11. White and White, *Friends & Friendship*, 33-8; Em Griffin, *Making Friends*, 141-2.

12. White and White, *Friends & Friendship*, 88-9; Conway, *Making Real Friends in a Phony World*, 36-7.

13. Inrig, *Quality Friendship*, 65.

14. Alan Loy McGinnis, *The Friendship Factor* (Minneapolis, Minn.: Augsburg, 1979), 29; White and White, *How to Make Friends*, 5-9.

15. Conway, *Making Real Friends in a Phony World*, 49.

16. McGinnis, *The Friendship Factor*, 68; White and White, *How to Make Friends*, 9-10.

17. McGinnis, *The Friendship Factor*, 63-5.

18. White and White, *How to Make Friends*, 11.

19. Henry Cloud and John Townsend, *Boundaries: When to Say Yes, When to Say No, To Take Control of Your Life* (Grand Rapids: Zondervan, 1992), 199–201.

20. Marie Chapian, *Growing Closer* (Old Tappan, N. J.: Fleming H. Revell, 1986), 19.

21. Inrig, *Quality Friendship*, 24-7.

22. McGinnis, *The Friendship Factor*, 123-4; White and White, *Friends & Friendship*, 88.

23. Conway, *Making Real Friends in a Phony World*, 39-40; Inrig, *Quality Friendship*, 24.

24. Chapian, *Growing Closer*, 160, 163; Conway, *Making Real Friends in a Phony World*, 92-3.

25. McGinnis, *The Friendship Factor*, 109-112; Conway, *Making Real Friends in a Phony World*, 88-115.

26. McGinnis, *The Friendship Factor*, 71; White and White, *How to Make Friends*, 18; Conway, *Making Real Friends in a Phony World*, 163-171.

27. Conway, *Making Real Friends in a Phony World*, 116-27.

28. Dale Carnegie, *How to Win Friends and Influence People* (New York: Pocket Books, 1940), 61.

29. White and White, *Friends & Friendship*, 61.

30. McGinnis, *The Friendship Factor*, 42; Conway, *Making Real Friends in a Phony World*, 124-6.

31. White and White, *How to Make Friends*, 14.

32. Conway, *Making Real Friends in a Phony World*, 40, 71.

33. McGinnis, *The Friendship Factor*, 68, 113; Conway, *Making Real Friends in a Phony World*, 70.

34. McGinnis, *The Friendship Factor*, 155.

35. White and White, *How to Make Friends*, 21; McGinnis, *The Friendship Factor*, 114; Conway, *Making Real Friends in a Phony World*, 75-6.

36. Chapian, *Growing Closer*, 52-3.

37. Chapian, *Growing Closer*, 59.

38. Crabb, *Understanding People*, 15–16; McGee, *The Search for Significance*, 27–30.

39. Inrig, *Quality Friendship*, 55-8, 73-104.

40. Swanson, *Dictionary of Biblical Languages,* electronic ed., #2876.

41. Dinah Maria Craik, *A Life for a Life*, vol. 1 (Leipzig: Berhnard Tauchnitz, 1859), 270.

HOPE FOR THE HEART TITLES

- *Adultery*
- *Aging Well*
- *Alcohol & Drug Abuse*
- *Anger*
- *Anorexia & Bulimia*
- *Boundaries*
- *Bullying*
- *Caregiving*
- *Chronic Illness & Disability*
- *Codependency*
- *Conflict Resolution*
- *Confrontation*
- *Considering Marriage*
- *Critical Spirit*
- *Decision Making*
- *Depression*
- *Domestic Violence*
- *Dysfunctional Family*
- *Envy & Jealousy*
- *Fear*
- *Financial Freedom*
- *Forgiveness*
- *Friendship*
- *Gambling*
- *Grief*
- *Guilt*
- *Hope*
- *Loneliness*
- *Manipulation*
- *Marriage*
- *Overeating*
- *Parenting*
- *Perfectionism*
- *Procrastination*
- *Reconciliation*
- *Rejection*
- *Self-Worth*
- *Sexual Integrity*
- *Singleness*
- *Spiritual Abuse*
- *Stress*
- *Success Through Failure*
- *Suicide Prevention*
- *Trials*
- *Verbal & Emotional Abuse*
- *Victimization*

www.hendricksonrose.com